SPECTRUM
EARLY YEARS

D1406456

Let's Learn to
TRACE

Published by Spectrum
an imprint of Carson-Dellosa Publishing LLC
Greensboro, NC

Spectrum
An imprint of Carson-Dellosa Publishing, LLC
P.O. Box 35665
Greensboro, NC 27425-5665

www.carsondellosa.com

Printed in Leominster, MA USA. All rights reserved.   ISBN 978-1-60996-199-2

1 2 3 4 5 6 7 8 9 10 QLM 17 16 15 14 13 12 11   349103711

Table of Contents

Welcome to the *Let's Learn* Series

The early years of your child's life are the most critical for development—both cognitively and physically. It is important that you nurture your child's growing interest in the world around him or her. It is also essential to prepare your child with the basic skills and fine motor skills necessary for the school years ahead. Basic skills include concepts such as the alphabet, numbers, colors, and shapes. Fine motor skills are movements that are produced by small muscles or muscle groups. Children in preschool spend a lot of their day developing these muscles in their hands. Developed motor skills are the key to success in school.

Young children learn best when they are actively involved in the learning process. *Let's Learn to Trace* features whimsical hands-on activities that children will love to complete. The act of tracing lines and shapes helps a child develop fine motor skills and hand-eye coordination.

Developing fine motor skills is also an important part of the brain development. Movement helps the organization of the brain. It reinforces growth and builds connections between different parts of the brain. More connections mean more brain power!

Help your child complete the activities in this book. There are directions for parents and simplified directions for the child. Allow your child to decipher and explore the activity on his or her own, but provide guidance when needed. Encourage your child to be as creative as possible when completing the activities. Most importantly, enjoy working through the book with your child. The time you invest in your child's development is priceless and will reap countless rewards for years to come.

Introduce your child to *Let's Learn to Trace* today and watch him or her succeed tomorrow!

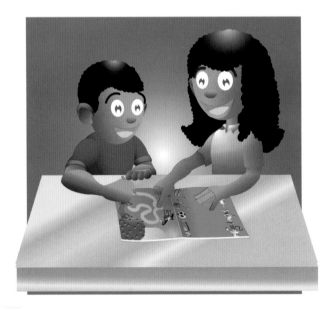

Tasty Treats

Skill: Tracing a straight line from left to right

Directions: Your child will help the animals get to their tasty treats! Before using a pencil to complete the activity, your child should trace the lines with his or her finger. This exercise helps your child's brain track and process what his or her hand is doing.

Trace from left to right.

Frog Jump

Skill: Tracing a curved line from left to right

Directions: Help your child count the jumps the frogs make in their race to the finish line! Your child should trace the lines with his or her finger before using a pencil to complete the activity. Which frog does your child think will come in first place? Which frog will come in last place?

Trace from left to right.

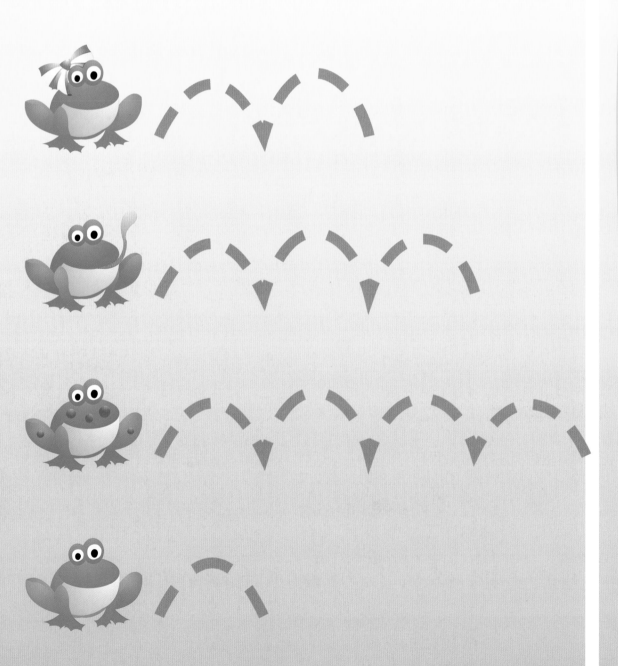

Gone Fishin'

Skill: Tracing a straight line from top to bottom

Directions: Your child will help the turtles catch some fish! Your child should trace the lines with his or her finger before using a pencil to complete the activity. This is your opportunity to talk to your child about the position words *top* and *bottom*. Show your child several visual examples of the position words.

Trace from top to bottom.

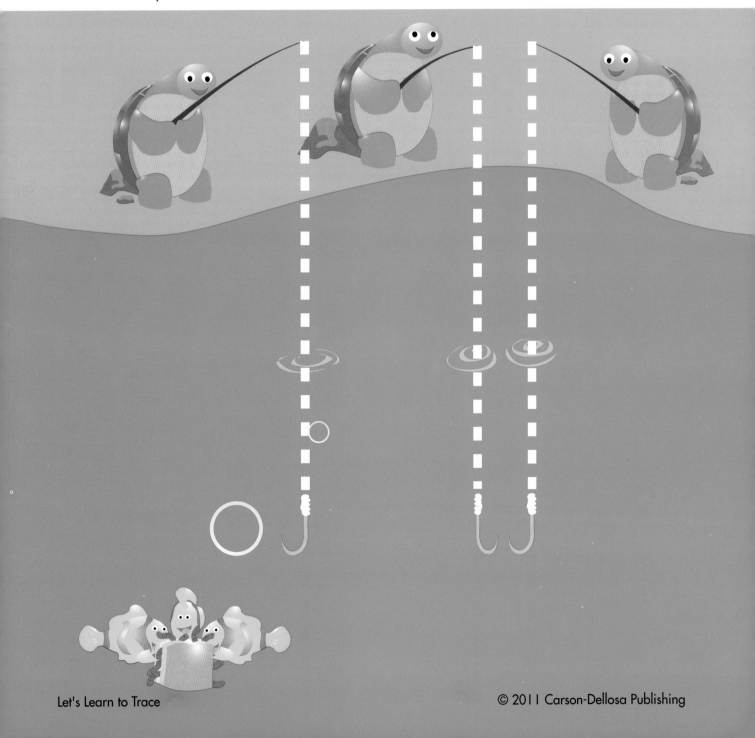

Seals on Slides

Skill: Tracing a zigzag line from top to bottom

Directions: Your child will help the seals ride to the bottom of the water slide. Which seal does your child think will reach the bottom first? Remember, your child should trace the lines with his or her finger before using a pencil to complete the activity.

Trace from top to bottom.

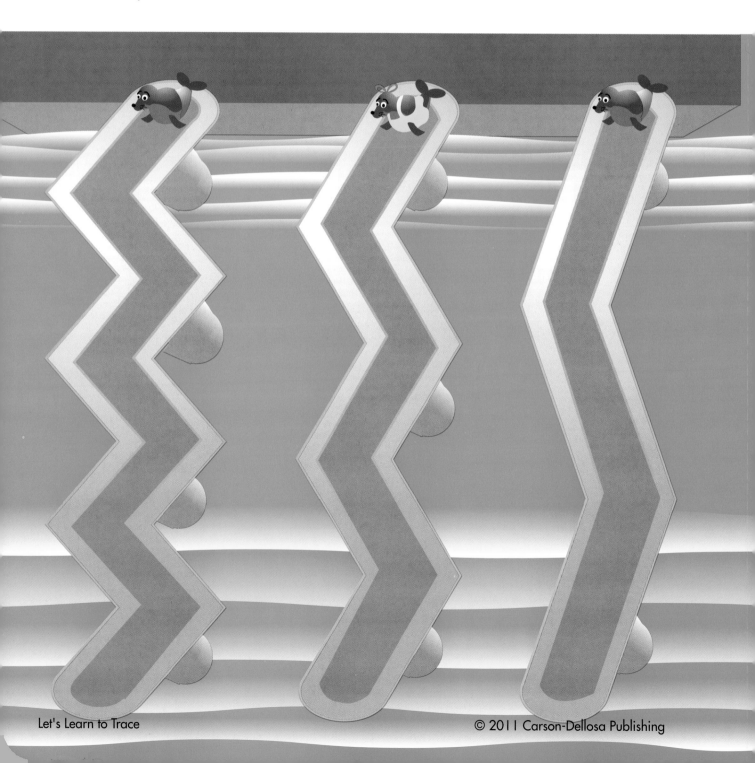

Hungry Bunny

Skill: Tracing a path

Directions: Help your child trace the bunny tracks to help the bunny get to the carrot. Show your child how to follow the path by moving from one set of bunny tracks to another. When your child is done with the activity, he or she can use the path to do the extension activity on page 61.

Trace a path.

Busy Bee

Skill: Tracing a path

Directions: Your child will follow the arrows to help the bee get to the flower. Remind your child to connect one arrow to the next as he or she traces the path. When your child is done with the activity, he or she can use the path to do the extension activity on page 61.

Trace a path.

Give a Dog a Bone

Skill: Tracing a path

Directions: Your child will start at the dog and trace the line to help the dog find the bone. When your child is done with the activity, he or she can use the path to do the extension activity on page 61.

Trace a path.

Wind-Blown Butterfly

Skill: Tracing a path

Directions: Your child will trace the line to help the butterfly get to the flower. When your child is done with the activity, he or she can use the path to do the extension activity on page 61.

Trace a path.

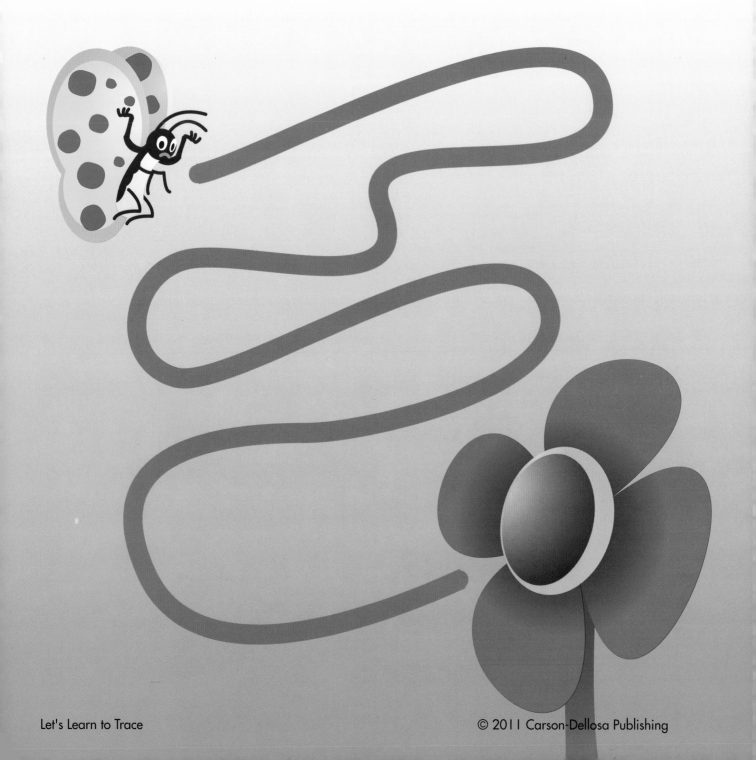

Fly Me to the Moon

Skill: Tracing a path

Directions: Tell your child to pretend that his or her pencil is a space shuttle that will carry the astronaut to the moon! When your child is done with the activity, he or she can use the path to do the extension activity on page 61.

Trace a path.

Jumbled Jump Ropes

Skill: Tracing a path

Directions: By tracing the lines, your child will help Kitty and Katie Kangaroo find the end of their jump ropes. Tell your child to trace the lines with his or her finger first.

Trace a path.

An Apple a Day

Skill: Tracing a path through a maze

Directions: Your child will complete the maze to help the horse get to the apple tree. Your child should trace the maze with his or her finger before using a pencil to complete the activity. When your child is done with the activity, he or she can use the maze to do the extension activity on page 61.

Complete the maze.

Acorn Treasure

Skill: Tracing a path through a maze

Directions: Your child will trace a path through the maze to help the squirrel get to the acorns. Your child should trace the maze with his or her finger before using a pencil to complete the activity. When your child is done with the activity, he or she can use the maze to do the extension activity on page 61.

Complete the maze.

Make Lemonade

Skill: Tracing a path through a maze

Directions: Your child will help the bear gather the ingredients needed for his lemonade stand. Encourage your child to use the pictures within the maze as clues. When your child is done with the activity, he or she can use the maze to do the extension activity on page 61.

Complete the maze.

Mud Bath

Skill: Tracing a path through a maze

Directions: Your child will trace a path through the maze to help the pig get to the mud bath. Your child should trace the maze with his or her finger before using a pencil to complete the activity. When your child is done with the activity, he or she can use the maze to do the extension activity on page 61.

Complete the maze.

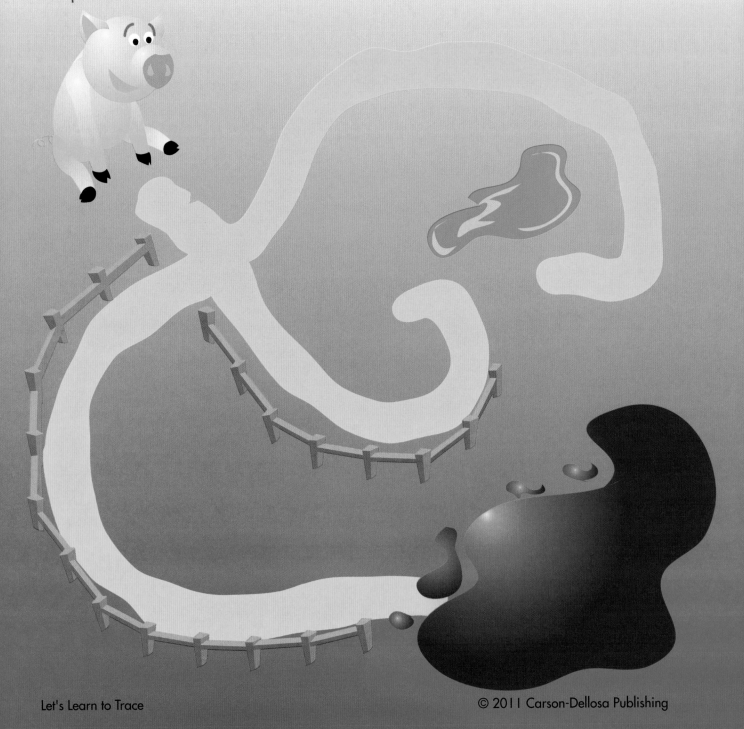

Fly Home

Skill: Tracing a path through a maze

Directions: Your child will trace a path through the maze to help the robin get to the nest. When your child is done with the activity, he or she can use the maze to do the extension activity on page 61.

Complete the maze.

Picnic Guest

Skill: Tracing a path through a maze

Directions: Your child will trace a path through the maze to help the ant get to the picnic basket. Because this maze is challenging, tell your child to trace the maze with his or her finger first. When your child is done with the activity, he or she can use the maze to do the extension activity on page 61.

Complete the maze.

A is for Apple

Skill: Tracing the letter **A**

Directions: Say the letter name out loud and have your child repeat you. What other words can your child think of that start with the same sound as *apple*? Remind your child to trace the letters with his or her finger before using a pencil to complete the activity.

Trace a letter.

A is for apple.

B is for Ball

Skill: Tracing the letter **B**

Directions: Say the letter name out loud and have your child repeat you. What other words can your child think of that start with the same sound as *ball*? Remind your child to trace the letters with his or her finger before using a pencil to complete the activity.

Trace a letter.

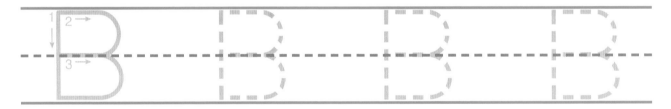

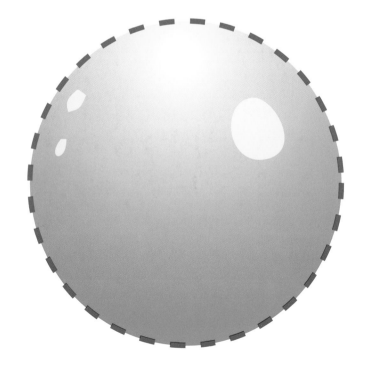

B is for ball.

C is for Car

Skill: Tracing the letter **C**

Directions: Say the letter name out loud and have your child repeat you. What other words can your child think of that start with the same sound as *car*? Remind your child to trace the letters with his or her finger before using a pencil to complete the activity.

Trace a letter.

C is for car.

D is for Duck

Skill: Tracing the letter **D**

Directions: Say the letter name out loud and have your child repeat you. What other words can your child think of that start with the same sound as *duck*? Remind your child to trace the letters with his or her finger before using a pencil to complete the activity.

Trace a letter.

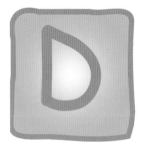

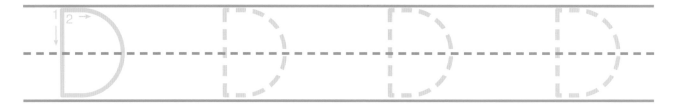

D is for duck.

E is for Egg

Skill: Tracing the letter **E**

Directions: Say the letter name out loud and have your child repeat you. What other words can your child think of that start with the same sound as *egg*? Remind your child to trace the letters with his or her finger before using a pencil to complete the activity.

Trace a letter.

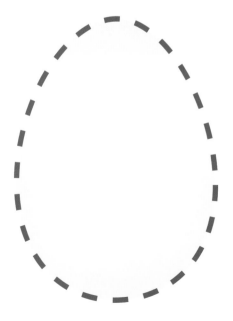

E is for egg.

F is for Football

Skill: Tracing the letter **F**

Directions: Say the letter name out loud and have your child repeat you. What other words can your child think of that start with the same sound as *football*? Remind your child to trace the letters with his or her finger before using a pencil to complete the activity.

Trace a letter.

F is for football.

G is for Guitar

Skill: Tracing the letter **G**

Directions: Say the letter name out loud and have your child repeat you. What other words can your child think of that start with the same sound as *guitar*? Remind your child to trace the letters with his or her finger before using a pencil to complete the activity.

Trace a letter.

G is for guitar.

H is for Hammer

Skill: Tracing the letter **H**

Directions: Say the letter name out loud and have your child repeat you. What other words can your child think of that start with the same sound as *hammer*? Remind your child to trace the letters with his or her finger before using a pencil to complete the activity.

Trace a letter.

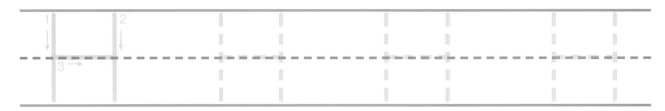

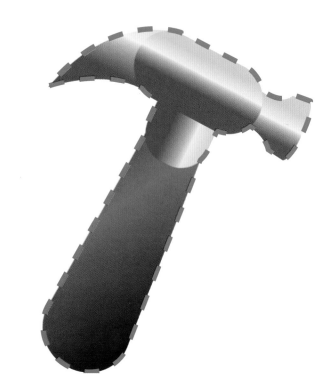

H is for hammer.

I is for Igloo

Skill: Tracing the letter **I**

Directions: Say the letter name out loud and have your child repeat you. What other words can your child think of that start with the same sound as *igloo*? Remind your child to trace the letters with his or her finger before using a pencil to complete the activity.

Trace a letter.

I is for igloo.

J is for Jellybean

Skill: Tracing the letter **J**

Directions: Say the letter name out loud and have your child repeat you. What other words can your child think of that start with the same sound as *jellybean*? Remind your child to trace the letters with his or her finger before using a pencil to complete the activity.

Trace a letter.

J is for jellybean.

K is for Kite

Skill: Tracing the letter **K**

Directions: Say the letter name out loud and have your child repeat you. What other words can your child think of that start with the same sound as *kite*? Remind your child to trace the letters with his or her finger before using a pencil to complete the activity.

Trace a letter.

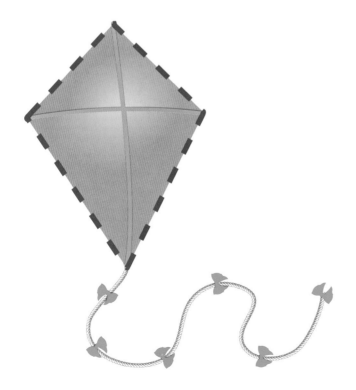

K is for kite.

L is for Lemon

Skill: Tracing the letter **L**

Directions: Say the letter name out loud and have your child repeat you. What other words can your child think of that start with the same sound as *lemon*? Remind your child to trace the letters with his or her finger before using a pencil to complete the activity.

Trace a letter.

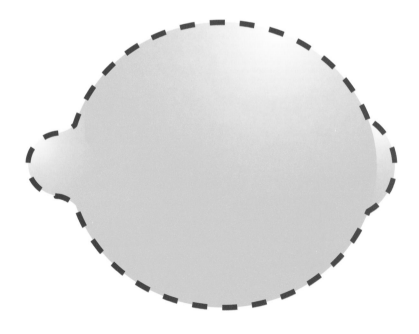

L is for lemon.

M **is for Mitten**

Skill: Tracing the letter **M**

Directions: Say the letter name out loud and have your child repeat you. What other words can your child think of that start with the same sound as *mitten*? Remind your child to trace the letters with his or her finger before using a pencil to complete the activity.

Trace a letter.

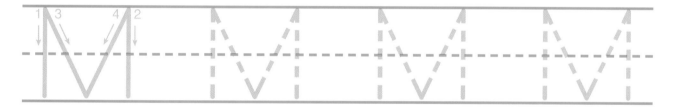

M **is for** mitten.

N is for Nest

Skill: Tracing the letter **N**

Directions: Say the letter name out loud and have your child repeat you. What other words can your child think of that start with the same sound as *nest*? Remind your child to trace the letters with his or her finger before using a pencil to complete the activity.

Trace a letter.

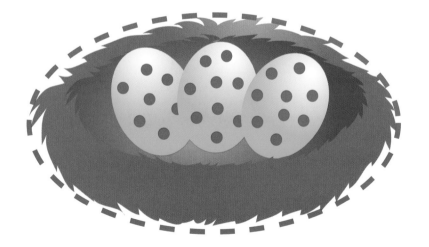

N is for nest.

O is for Orange

Skill: Tracing the letter **O**

Directions: Say the letter name out loud and have your child repeat you. What other words can your child think of that start with the same sound as *orange*? Remind your child to trace the letters with his or her finger before using a pencil to complete the activity.

Trace a letter.

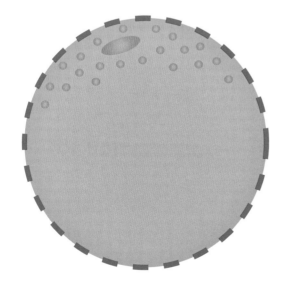

O is for orange.

P is for Pear

Skill: Tracing the letter **P**

Directions: Say the letter name out loud and have your child repeat you. What other words can your child think of that start with the same sound as *pear*? Remind your child to trace the letters with his or her finger before using a pencil to complete the activity.

Trace a letter.

P is for pear.

Q is for Quilt

Skill: Tracing the letter **Q**

Directions: Say the letter name out loud and have your child repeat you. What other words can your child think of that start with the same sound as *quilt*? Remind your child to trace the letters with his or her finger before using a pencil to complete the activity.

Trace a letter.

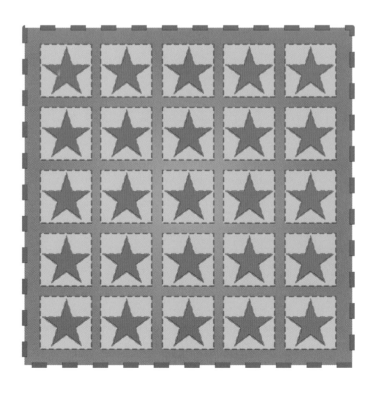

Q is for quilt.

R **is for Rainbow**

Skill: Tracing the letter **R**

Directions: Say the letter name out loud and have your child repeat you. What other words can your child think of that start with the same sound as *rainbow*? Remind your child to trace the letters with his or her finger before using a pencil to complete the activity.

Trace a letter.

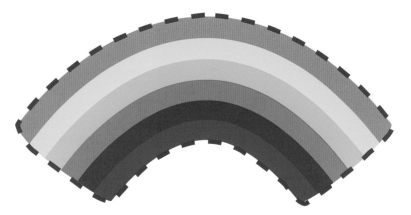

R is for rainbow.

S is for Sun

Skill: Tracing the letter **S**

Directions: Say the letter name out loud and have your child repeat you. What other words can your child think of that start with the same sound as *sun*? Remind your child to trace the letters with his or her finger before using a pencil to complete the activity.

Trace a letter.

S is for sun.

T is for Tent

Skill: Tracing the letter **T**

Directions: Say the letter name out loud and have your child repeat you. What other words can your child think of that start with the same sound as *tent*? Remind your child to trace the letters with his or her finger before using a pencil to complete the activity.

Trace a letter.

T is for tent.

U is for Umbrella

Skill: Tracing the letter **U**

Directions: Say the letter name out loud and have your child repeat you. What other words can your child think of that start with the same sound as *umbrella*? Remind your child to trace the letters with his or her finger before using a pencil to complete the activity.

Trace a letter.

U is for umbrella.

V is for Vase

Skill: Tracing the letter **V**

Directions: Say the letter name out loud and have your child repeat you. What other words can your child think of that start with the same sound as *vase*? Remind your child to trace the letters with his or her finger before using a pencil to complete the activity.

Trace a letter.

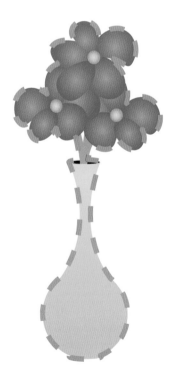

V is for vase.

W is for Wagon

Skill: Tracing the letter **W**

Directions: Say the letter name out loud and have your child repeat you. What other words can your child think of that start with the same sound as *wagon*? Remind your child to trace the letters with his or her finger before using a pencil to complete the activity.

Trace a letter.

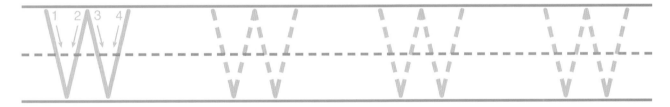

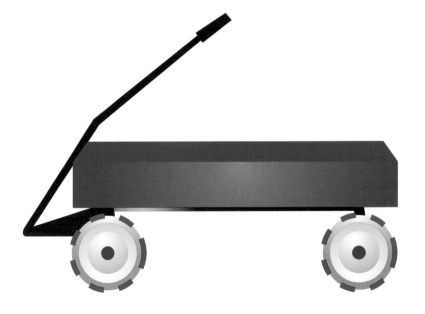

W is for wagon.

X is for Box

Skill: Tracing the letter **X**

Directions: Say the letter name out loud and have your child repeat you. What other words can your child think of that end with the same sound as *box*? Remind your child to trace the letters with his or her finger before using a pencil to complete the activity.

Trace a letter.

X is for box.

Y is for Yo-Yo

Skill: Tracing the letter **Y**

Directions: Say the letter name out loud and have your child repeat you. What other words can your child think of that start with the same sound as *yo-yo*? Remind your child to trace the letters with his or her finger before using a pencil to complete the activity.

Trace your name.

Y is for yo-yo.

Z is for Zoo

Skill: Tracing the letter **Z**

Directions: Say the letter name out loud and have your child repeat you. What other words can your child think of that start with the same sound as zoo? Remind your child to trace the letters with his or her finger before using a pencil to complete the activity.

Trace a letter.

Z is for zoo.

Trace Your Name

Skill: Tracing a name

Directions: Use a pencil to write your child's name on the line at the top of the page. Then, encourage your child to trace over the letters with his or her finger. Next, have your child trace the letters with a darker-colored pencil. You can also look at page 61 for the extension for this activity.

Trace your name.

© 2011 Carson-Dellosa Publishing

One and Two

Skill: Tracing and counting numbers **1** and **2**

Directions: Say each number out loud with your child. Have your child trace the numbers with his or her finger first. Then, he or she will use a pencil to complete the activity. When your child is done tracing, have your child touch the number words as you say them. Then, help your child count the dots on each die.

Trace a number. Say the word. Count the dots.

one

two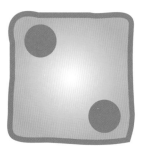

Three and Four

Skill: Tracing and counting numbers **3** and **4**

Directions: Say each number out loud with your child. Have your child trace the numbers with his or her finger first. Then, he or she will use a pencil to complete the activity. When your child is done tracing, have your child touch the number words as you say them. Then, help your child count the dots on each die.

Trace a number. Say the word. Count the dots.

three

four

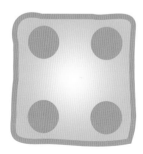

Five and Six

Skill: Tracing and counting numbers **5** and **6**

Directions: Say each number out loud with your child. Have your child trace the numbers with his or her finger first. Then, he or she will use a pencil to complete the activity. When your child is done tracing, have your child touch the number words as you say them. Then, help your child count the dots on each die.

Trace a number. Say the word. Count the dots.

five

six

Seven and Eight

Skill: Tracing and counting numbers **7** and **8**

Directions: Say each number out loud with your child. Have your child trace the numbers with his or her finger first. Then, he or she will use a pencil to complete the activity. When your child is done tracing, have your child touch the number words as you say them. Then, help your child count the dots on each die.

Trace a number. Say the word. Count the dots.

 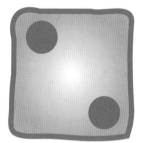

seven

eight

Nine and Ten

Skill: Tracing and counting numbers **9** and **10**

Directions: Say each number out loud with your child. Have your child trace the numbers with his or her finger first. Then, he or she will use a pencil to complete the activity. When your child is done tracing, have your child touch the number words as you say them. Then, help your child count the dots on each die.

Trace a number. Say the word. Count the dots.

nine

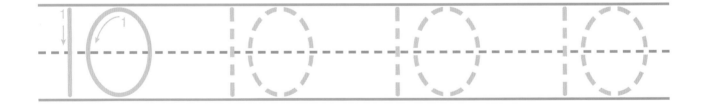

ten

Beary Nice Snowman

Skill: Tracing a circle

Directions: Starting at the dots, your child will trace the circles to help the bears finish the snowman. Your child should trace the circles with his or her finger before using a pencil to complete the activity.

Trace a circle.

Planets

Skill: Tracing a circle

Directions: Starting at the dots, your child will finish the planets by tracing the circles. Suggest that he or she trace the circles with his or her finger first. Name the planets for your child, and help him or her count all the planets on the page.

Trace a circle.

Venus

Earth

Mars

Jupiter

Pig's Brick House

Skill: Tracing a square

Directions: Your child will trace the squares on Pig's house to finish the windows. He or she should trace the squares with his or her finger before using a pencil to complete the activity. Ask your child if this picture reminds him or her of a fairy tale. Which one?

Trace a square.

Rabbit's Scrapbook

Skill: Tracing a square

Directions: Your child will trace the photographs to help Rabbit finish his scrapbook. He or she will use the dots as starting points and trace around all the squares. Can your child count how many pictures are in Rabbit's scrapbook?

Trace a square.

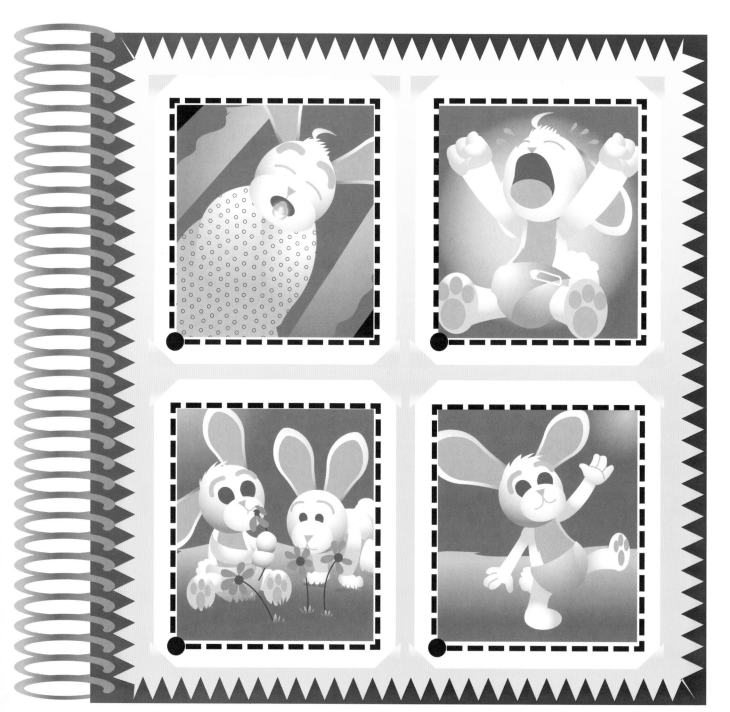

Sailboat Race

Skill: Tracing a triangle

Directions: Starting at the dots, your child will trace the triangles on the boats to finish the picture. Your child should trace the triangles with his or her finger before using a pencil to complete the activity. Can your child guess which sailboat will win the race?

Trace a triangle.

Pizza Time

Skill: Tracing a triangle

Directions: Your child will trace the pizza slice on the plate to finish the picture. Ask your child if he or she can find another triangle on the page to trace.

Trace a triangle.

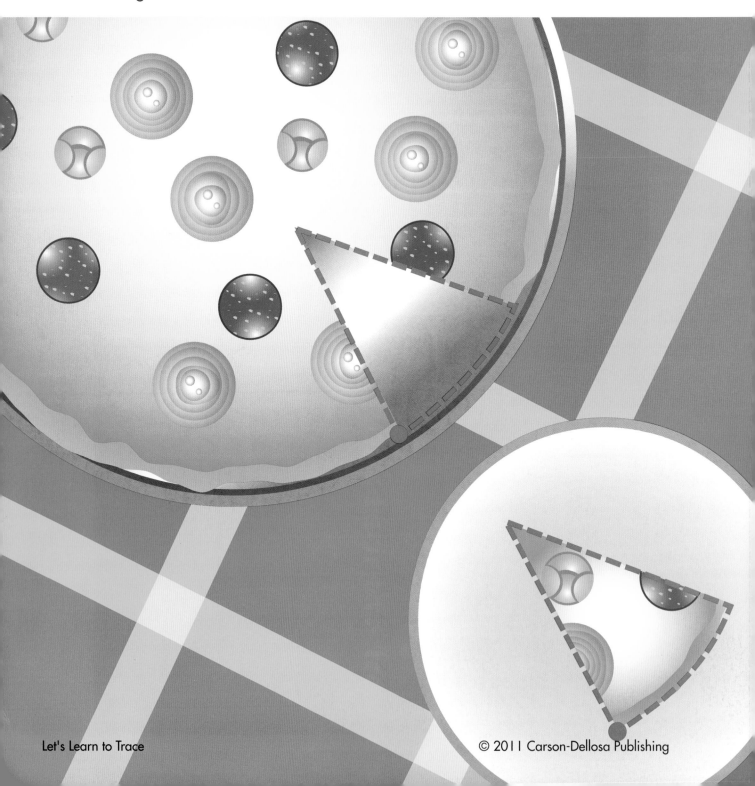

Big Buildings

Skill: Tracing a rectangle

Directions: Your child will trace the buildings to finish the picture of the city. Starting at the dot, he or she should trace the rectangles with his or her finger before using a pencil to complete the activity. Can your child tell you which building is tallest? Or shortest?

Trace a rectangle.

Pretty Presents

Skill: Tracing a rectangle

Directions: Your child will trace the rectangles to reveal the pretty presents. Tell your child to use his or her imagination to guess what gift could be in each package.

Trace a rectangle.

Extension Activities for Tracing

Use the following hands-on activities to enhance your child's fine motor development. Keep in mind that the process, not the finished product, is what is important. Work beside your child and model various tracing activities for him or her.

Maze Magic

This activity will help your child stay between the lines when completing a maze. Use the maze activities in this book or draw your own maze. Then, trace the lines of the maze with raised craft paint or glue. When the paint or glue is dry, give the maze to your child to complete. The raised paint or glue will serve as a "bumper" for your child's pencil, keeping his or her pencil within the boundaries of the maze.

Path to Success

Place small objects, such as buttons, beads, stones, or bits of cereal, on a piece of white paper. Label one object "Start" and another object "End." Your child will trace a path that circles every object on the page and stops at the end. See how many different paths your child can come up with. He or she can use a different color for each path. (Safety Tip: Never leave your child alone with small objects.)

Tracing Away

Find household objects for your child to trace that are the same shape as the shapes in the activities. Some examples include coasters, combs, mugs or glasses, and photographs. Ask your child to identify the shape of each object before he or she begins to trace it.

Trace Your Name

After completing Activity #43, give your child additional practice tracing his or her name. Using a pencil, write your child's name in big letters. Your child will use alternating colors of crayons, colored pencils, or markers to trace the letters of his or her name.

Color Resist

Give your child a white crayon and a white piece of paper. Have your child press down hard as he or she traces around different objects. He or she can overlap the shapes to create a more interesting design. Then, mix colored tempera paint with water for your child to brush over his or her drawing. As the wax resists the paint, your child's creation will begin to appear. Your child can also use colored crayons with this activity.

Fingers and Toes

Trace around your child's hands or feet. Then, have your child color the picture. You can write the date on the paper and save it in a memory box. You can also let your child trace around your hands and feet.

Ruler Design

Your child will lay a ruler down on a piece of paper, trace a line, then move the ruler and trace another line. Your child will repeat this process to create a piece of art. Model how to hold the ruler down with one hand and trace with the other. You may have to hold the ruler down as your child draws.

What's That Object?

Place five or six household objects on a tray. You can use cookie cutters, mixing spoons, CDs, or anything else you can think of. Have your child look away as you trace around one of the objects and place it back on the tray. Then, your child will try to guess which object you traced. Take turns tracing and guessing.

Magnet Experiment

Provide your child with an assortment of magnets, items that can be attracted to magnets, and items that cannot be attracted to magnets. Have your child test the items and sort all the objects into two piles. Give your child a piece of paper and ask him or her to trace the objects that can be attracted to magnets.